# 100%
# PURE
# FAKE

## LYN THOMAS

with photographs by Cheryl Powers
and illustrations by Boris Zaytsev

## KIDS CAN PRESS

*I'd like to dedicate this book to my daughter, Emma. During the experimentation and writing of this book, she constantly reminded me of the fun times she had as a kid feeling grossed out with "weird" stuff!*

*Also to Chloe Scaber, my little helper, and her sister, Payton, who was at the receiving end of some of the 100% Pure Fakes. Edible doo-doos were particularly well received, with much gagging. — L.T.*

**Acknowledgments**
As always, thanks to my great pal and editor extraordinaire, Val Wyatt. We both had a lot of fun with this book. It's not often you can be your average 10-year-old all over again. I would also like to acknowledge all the folks at KCP who helped with this book, especially designer Karen Powers, photographer Cheryl Powers and the kids who acted as models.

Kids Can Press acknowledges the financial support of the Government of Ontario, through the Ontario Media Development Corporation's Ontario Book Initiative, and the Government of Canada, through the BPIDP, for our publishing activity.

Published in Canada by
Kids Can Press Ltd
29 Birch Avenue
Toronto, ON  M4V 1E2

Published in the U.S. by
Kids Can Press Ltd.
2250 Military Road
Tonawanda, NY  14150

www.kidscanpress.com

Edited by Valerie Wyatt
Designed by Karen Powers
Cover photography by Cheryl Powers
Printed and bound in Singapore

This book is smyth sewn casebound.

CM 09  0 9 8 7 6 5 4 3 2 1

**Library and Archives Canada Cataloguing in Publication**

Thomas, Lyn, 1949–
    100% pure fake : gross out your friends and family with 25 great special effects! / written by Lyn Thomas.

ISBN 978-1-55453-290-2

1. Scientific recreations—Juvenile literature. 2. Science—Experiments—Juvenile literature. I. Title.  II. Title: One hundred percent pure fake.

Q164.T48 2009          j793.8          C2008-908108-0

Kids Can Press is a  Entertainment company

# CONTENTS

What This Book Is All About .................. 4

Keeping It Safe ............................. 6

100% Pure Fake Blood ...................... 8

Scars and Blisters ......................... 12

Scar Face ................................. 14

Rotting Skin .............................. 16

The Hairy Mole ........................... 18

S'not Snot ................................ 20

Oddball Eyeballs .......................... 24

Brain Pie ................................. 26

Shrunken Heads ........................... 28

Severed Finger ............................ 30

Broken Glass ............................. 32

Chocolate Milk Spill ...................... 34

Slimy Worms ............................. 36

Road Kill Guts ........................... 38

Veggie Vomit ............................. 40

Edible Barf ............................... 42

Cat and Dog Doo-Doos .................... 44

Edible Doo-Doos .......................... 46

Puddle of Pee ............................ 48

# WHAT this BOOK IS All ABOUT

Fun, that's what! And what could be more fun than astonishing your friends and family with 100% Pure Fake snot, edible dog doo-doos, drink spills or the rest of the fantastic 100% Pure Fakes in this book? Not much, really.

Our 100% Pure Fake kid-tested projects are guaranteed to cause amazing and sometimes alarming responses from your family and friends.

4

# Mess alert

Making Pure Fakes can be messy. Before you start, cover your work area with a layer of newspapers and put on an apron or old shirt.

# Working with food coloring

Always start with a very small amount of the coloring — you can always add more, but you can't take it away. The best way to control the amount is to dip the tip of a paintbrush into the food coloring and then into the mixture you want to color. Keep dipping and adding until you have the color you want. If you can't find black food coloring, mix drops of blue, red and green together.

 **WARNING**: Food coloring may stain. Follow the Mess Alert above.

# Working with gelatin

Some Pure Fakes use gelatin, which can be bought in a grocery store. Once gelatin is mixed with water, it starts to set, so work quickly and follow the instructions for each project. If it sets too much, put your bowl of gelatin into another bowl of hot water and stir until it softens again.

 **READ THIS**: Once you've finished making stuff with gelatin, such as the snot or scars, throw it into the garbage, not down the sink.

5

# Keeping It SAFE

*You'll notice that some of the projects have warning symbols. PAY ATTENTION TO THEM!*

Guess I should have paid attention to those warnings.

**ALLERGY ALERT!!!**

*Contains peanuts and cocoa*

If you have allergies, look for this symbol.

**HOT LIQUIDS**

*GET ADULT HELP*

Ask an adult to help anytime you are working with hot liquids.

**HOT STOVE**

*GET ADULT HELP*

Ditto for using the stove.

**WARNING!**

This symbol has important safety information.

---

### ONE MORE THING

*Don't eat any 100% Pure Fakes unless you're told it's okay to do so, and don't eat anything that's been sitting around unrefrigerated.*

# Tips

Look for the blue hand. It points out special tips to make the most of your 100% Pure Fakes.

# And finally ...

Most Pure Fakes in the book can be made out of stuff that's already in your kitchen. Other ingredients, such as school glue, tempera paint and gelatin, are widely available in grocery or craft stores.

We hope you have as much fun making the 100% Pure Fakes as we did coming up with them.

## OUR VERY BEST ADVICE

* Assemble all your ingredients first.
* Read the instructions before you start.
* Practice makes perfect.
* And take those safety and mess precautions seriously.

# 100% PURE FAKE

# BLOOD

*Let's face it — as an attention-getter, nothing beats fake blood. Here's one simple recipe that can be transformed into three gory blood mixtures that'll get a lot of attention.*

**BE SURE TO READ THIS FIRST!**

Fake blood is really messy, and the food coloring in it will stain clothing and carpets. So before you start

✱ cover your work surface with newspaper

✱ wear old clothes or an apron

# Your Basic Blood

This basic blood is thin and drippy, like blood from a finger cut or scratch. Pour a small amount on your hand or arm and watch it dribble down. Moan a bit and ask for a Band-Aid.

**STUFF YOU'LL NEED:**
- 125 mL (½ c.) corn syrup
- 5 mL (1 tsp.) red food coloring
- 3 to 4 drops of blue food coloring

# What to do:

**1** Pour the corn syrup into a bowl. Add the food coloring. Mix well. Ta-da! Fake blood.

OooH!!! The PAiN!

## The Creepy Cut Artery Effect

Blood that flows through arteries is darker than your bright red Basic Blood. To make arterial blood, put 15 mL (1 tbsp.) of Basic Blood into a clean bowl. Add a few drops of green food coloring. Drip some of this blood onto your neck and wait for someone to scream.

## The Scraped Elbow or Knee Effect

With a Popsicle stick, smear some Basic Blood onto your knee or elbow. Sprinkle on some dry coffee grounds. Blow away the excess. Presto — road rash without the pain.

# The Blood Clot Effect

Old blood forms sticky clots. Here's how to make some.

**1** Mix together 5 mL (1 tsp.) crunchy peanut butter and 2.5 mL (½ tsp.) cocoa powder in a bowl.

**2** Add 15 mL (1 tbsp.) of Basic Blood from page 9 and 1 to 2 drops of red food coloring.

**ALLERGY ALERT!!!**

Contains peanuts and cocoa

*TIP:* Smear the blood on your hand. Show a friend and tell her you just haven't had time to clean it up. Then lick it. Yep. Lick it. It's edible.

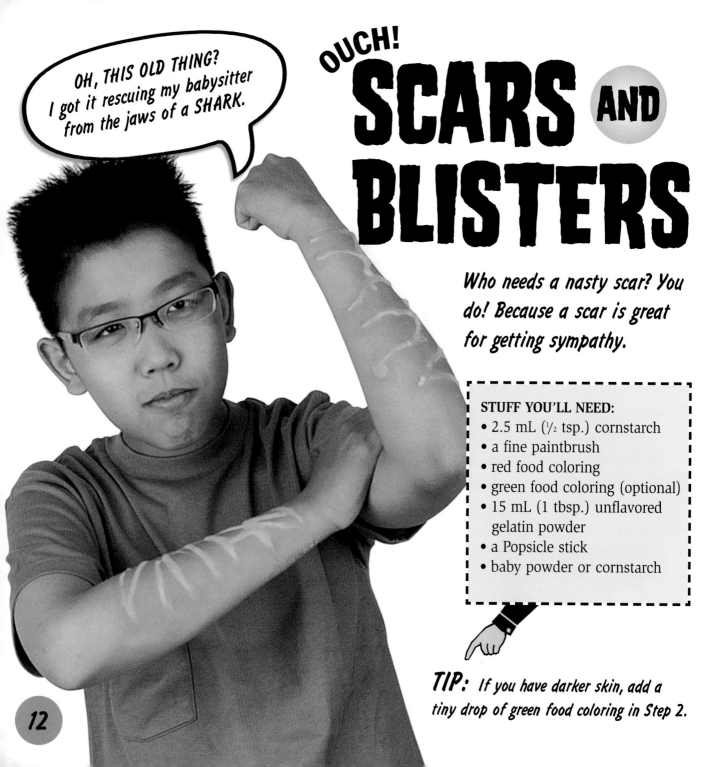

OH, THIS OLD THING? I got it rescuing my babysitter from the jaws of a SHARK.

OUCH!
# SCARS AND BLISTERS

*Who needs a nasty scar? You do! Because a scar is great for getting sympathy.*

**STUFF YOU'LL NEED:**
- 2.5 mL (½ tsp.) cornstarch
- a fine paintbrush
- red food coloring
- green food coloring (optional)
- 15 mL (1 tbsp.) unflavored gelatin powder
- a Popsicle stick
- baby powder or cornstarch

*TIP:* If you have darker skin, add a tiny drop of green food coloring in Step 2.

# What to do:

**HOT LIQUIDS**
***GET ADULT HELP***

**1** Mix the cornstarch with 2.5 mL (½ tsp.) cold water.

**2** Squeeze a few drops of red food coloring onto a small dish. Dip the tip of the paintbrush into the food coloring and stir it into the cornstarch mixture to get a milky pink color. Add more food coloring if needed.

**3** Ask an adult to pour 30 mL (2 tbsp.) boiling water into a measuring cup. Add the gelatin powder. Stir quickly for about 15 seconds, until the gelatin is dissolved.

**4** Add the cornstarch mixture to the gelatin and stir again.

**5** Put the mixture in the fridge and wait about 10 minutes, until it's thick but not set. Get ready to work quickly.

**6** Use the Popsicle stick to put long thin stripes of the mixture on your arm. Instant scars.

**7** Sprinkle some baby powder or cornstarch onto the scar. Blow away the excess. Clean the edges of the scar with a paper towel. CONGRATULATIONS! You are now the owner of an excellent (but completely fake) scar.

# Blister

*You can use the same recipe to make an amazing blister.*

**1** Put a blob of the mixture from Step 5 on your skin.

**2** Tear a small piece of bathroom tissue just big enough to cover the blob. Put the tissue on the wet blob. The tissue will soak up the liquid.

**3** Pinch the tissue to make it lumpy in the center. Smooth the edges of your blister. Wipe the edges clean. Lovely!

13

# SCAR FACE

*Apply goop. Let dry. Scare the pants off friends and family. Get a friend to help — this recipe makes enough for two.*

**TIP:** *If you have darker skin, add a tiny drop of green food coloring in Step 3.*

**STUFF YOU'LL NEED:**
- 30 mL (2 tbsp.) unflavored gelatin powder
- 45 mL (3 tbsp.) milk
- red food coloring
- green food coloring (optional)
- a fine paintbrush
- baby powder
- a sponge or cotton ball

# What to do:

**! HOT LIQUIDS**

**GET ADULT HELP**

**1** Pour 30 mL (2 tbsp.) cold water into a small bowl and sprinkle the gelatin powder over top. Do not stir.

**2** Ask an adult to bring the milk to a boil on the stove. Pour the milk into the bowl with the gelatin mixture and stir until the gelatin is dissolved.

**3** Squeeze a few drops of red food coloring onto a small dish. Dip the tip of the paintbrush into the food coloring and stir it into the gelatin mixture until it is barely pink. You only want a touch of pink.

**4** Stir the mixture until it is still slightly liquid but also has some lumps. This will take up to 8 minutes. It should be *just about* firm, but still liquid enough to smear on your face. Go ahead and smear or have a friend do it for you.

**5** Once you look sufficiently creepy, pat on some baby powder with a sponge or cotton ball. Have your friend blow away the excess powder.

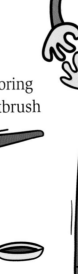

***TIP:*** *This stuff sets almost like rubber and, if you're careful, you can peel it off and use it again. Or, to get rid of it, wash your face with soap and water.*

# ROTTING SKIN

It takes a bit of fiddling to get the crusty, creepy look of rotting skin just right, but it's definitely worth the effort. Ask a friend to help you — it's easier (and more fun) with two people.

MOM, I washed with that new soap and LOOK what happened!

**WARNING!**

*If you are making rotting skin on your face, don't use a hair dryer.*

# What to do:

**1** Put the glue in a bowl and add 2 to 3 drops of the food coloring. Stir to mix. You should have a nice, black goopy mixture.

**2** Put the rolled oats in another bowl and mix in the corn syrup.

**3** Dab some of the black mixture onto your arm with a cotton ball. Let it dry. Using a hair dryer set on LOW will speed things up, but make sure to hold the dryer at least 15 cm (6 in.) away from your skin.

**4** Use a Popsicle stick to add a layer of the rolled oats mixture. The black should show through. Dab a bit more of the black mixture on top of the oats, if you wish.

**5** Let the patch of rotting skin dry so that when you pat it, the rolled oats stay put. This will take a while, so be patient. Using a hair dryer set on LOW will help.

**6** When your rotting skin is dry, use a clean cotton ball to pat on some of the liquid face makeup. Do a little at a time. When you're finished, some of the black color should peek through.

# THE HAIRY MOLE

A MOLE smack in the middle of your face is a nice accessory for Halloween. Not a real mole, but a great BIG, HAIRY FAKE one.

**STUFF YOU'LL NEED:**
- 5 mL (1 tsp.) corn syrup
- 5 mL (1 tsp.) cocoa powder
- 3 pieces of hair from your head, each about 2 cm (³⁄₄ in.) long

## What to do:

**1** Pour the corn syrup into a small bowl. Add the cocoa power. Stir until well mixed and gooey.

**2** Put a small blob of the mixture on your cheek.

**3** Gently stick the hairs into the blob on your face.

Congratulations! You're the proud owner of a 100% Pure Fake hairy mole.

Your mole goo can be kept for a day or so in a bowl, covered with plastic wrap.

*TIP: Make another blob on your face and stick a peppercorn into it to make it look more crusty.*

# The Hairy Wart

*If you're in grade six, you've probably already tried this. But just in case ...*

**STUFF YOU'LL NEED:**
- a pencil with an eraser on top
- a few strands of hair from your head
- double-sided tape

## What to do:

**1** Remove the eraser from the pencil and ask an adult to cut a small slit in it with a knife, like this:

**2** Pinch the eraser to open the slit and stick in a few hairs.

**3** Use double-sided tape to stick the wart to your hand or other body part.

*19*

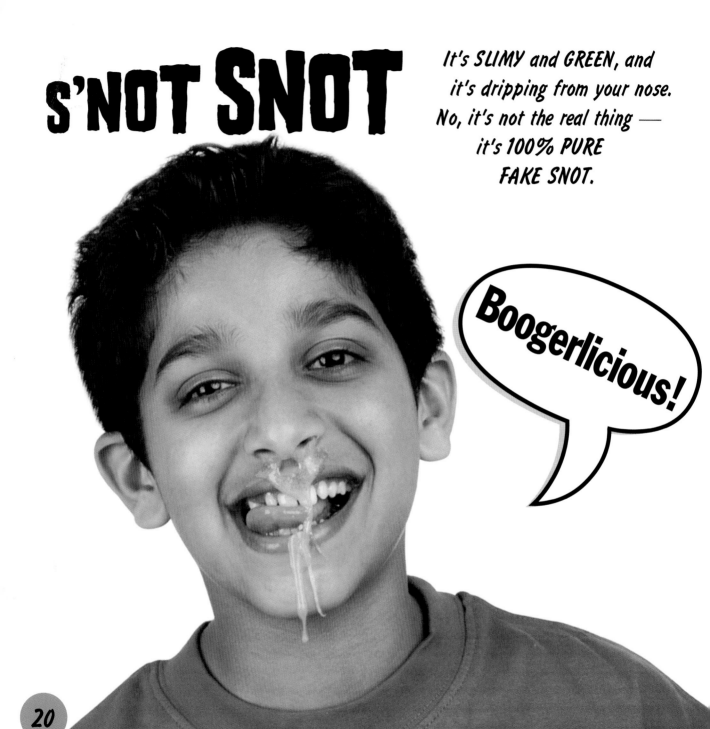

# Pure Snot

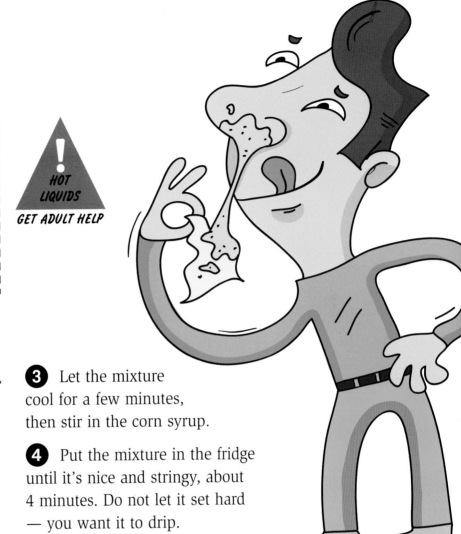

**HOT LIQUIDS**
*GET ADULT HELP*

# What to do:

**1** Ask an adult to pour 15 mL (1 tbsp.) of boiling water into a measuring cup. Add the gelatin powder. Stir quickly for about 15 seconds, until the gelatin is dissolved.

**2** Squeeze a few drops of green food coloring onto a small dish. Dip the tip of the paintbrush into the food coloring and stir it into the gelatin mixture. You only want a touch of green.

**3** Let the mixture cool for a few minutes, then stir in the corn syrup.

**4** Put the mixture in the fridge until it's nice and stringy, about 4 minutes. Do not let it set hard — you want it to drip.

*TIP:* Put some of the snot mix in a tissue or handkerchief. Pretend to blow your nose and, while you're doing so, rub the snot on your nose and lips. It's DRIPPY and DISGUSTING.

# Lumpy Snot

*If you think the slimy snot from page 20 is DISGUSTING, wait until you try this LUMPY version.*

## What to do:

**!** HOT LIQUIDS

**GET ADULT HELP**

**1** Pour 30 mL (2 tbsp.) cold water into a small bowl and sprinkle the gelatin powder over top. Do not stir.

**2** Ask an adult to bring the milk to a boil on the stove. Pour the milk into the bowl with the gelatin mixture and stir until the gelatin is dissolved.

**3** Squeeze a few drops of green food coloring onto a small dish. Dip the tip of the paintbrush into the food coloring and stir it into the gelatin mixture. You only want a touch of green.

**4** This is the tricky part. Stir until lumps start to form. The mixture should still be slightly liquid. This will take about 8 minutes, but try a bit of it as soon as you see lumps forming. Make sure mixture is cool before putting it on your face. Smear some at the base of your nostrils. Lovely! Instant lumpy snot.

# What to do with your 100% Pure Fake snot

✱ With your snot in place, walk into a room full of people and ask if anyone has a tissue. Watch them flinch.

✱ To make a booger you can play with, wait just a few more minutes for the mixture to set more in Step 4. Put a small amount in the palm of your hand. Pretend to sneeze or cough it up. Say, "Sorry," then open your hand and start playing with your booger.

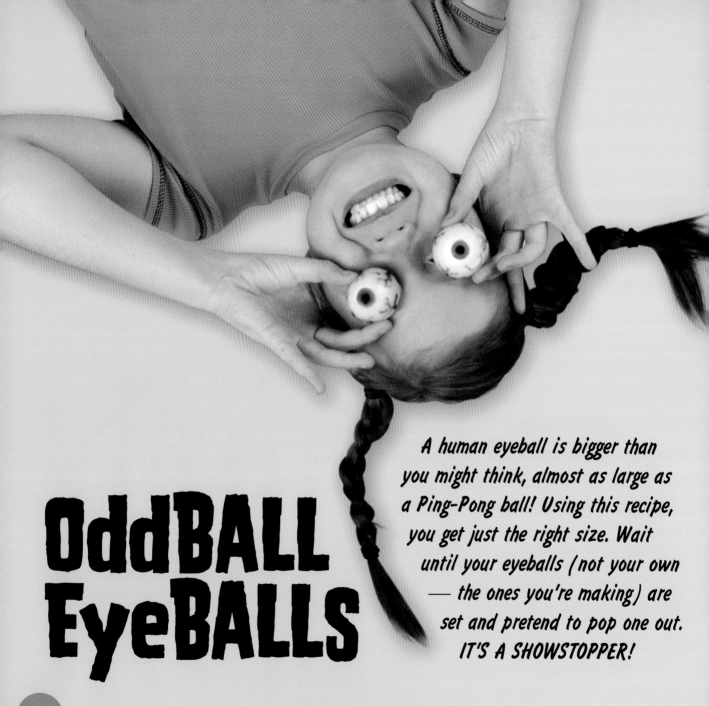

# OddBALL EyeBALLS

A human eyeball is bigger than you might think, almost as large as a Ping-Pong ball! Using this recipe, you get just the right size. Wait until your eyeballs (not your own — the ones you're making) are set and pretend to pop one out. *IT'S A SHOWSTOPPER!*

**STUFF YOU'LL NEED:**
- 2 uncooked eggs
- 15 mL (1 tbsp.) unflavored gelatin powder
- 2.5 mL (½ tsp.) cornstarch
- red and blue food coloring
- black food coloring (or mix blue, red and green)
- a fine paintbrush

HOT LIQUIDS

**GET ADULT HELP**

# What to do:

**1** Ask an adult to boil the eggs for about 3 minutes, then rinse them under cold water. Have the adult crack the top third of the shell off the pointed end of each egg and scoop out the insides. The empty eggshells will be your eyeball molds.

**2** Put each shell in an egg cup to keep it steady.

**3** Ask an adult to pour 50 mL (3 tbsp.) of boiling water into a measuring cup. Add the gelatin powder. Stir quickly for about 15 seconds, until the gelatin is dissolved.

**4** Add the cornstarch. Mix well to get rid of the lumps.

**5** Pour equal amounts of the mixture into the two eggshells. Let them set in the fridge for about an hour.

**6** Once the gelatin is firm, carefully peel away the eggshells to reveal two lovely eyeballs.

**7** Now the fun starts. Dip the paintbrush into the blue food coloring and paint a circle on the rounded part of the eye to make the iris. When it is dry, paint on a pupil with black food coloring. Paint some fine lines of red food coloring to look like broken blood vessels.

## WHAT TO DO WITH YOUR CREEPY EYEBALLS

✱ Gel your hair and make it stand up. Hold your fake eyeballs up to your own eyes and leap out from behind a door when someone walks by.

✱ Put the fake eyeballs side by side in a bathroom cupboard or staring up from a drawer.

# BRAIN PIE

Tired of apple and pumpkin pie?
Why not serve up a 100% PURE FAKE brain pie!
It's not edible, but it IS an attention-getter.

!
HOT
LIQUIDS

GET ADULT HELP

- 750 mL (3 c.) precooked udon noodles or thick spaghetti cooked, rinsed and drained
- red and green food coloring
- 30 mL (2 tbsp.) milk
- 30 mL (2 tbsp.) unflavored gelatin powder

# What to do:

**1** Find a bowl that's just big enough to fit over the top part of your head. That way your brain will be the right size. Line the bowl with a layer of aluminum foil. Next, crinkle up 10 strips of foil and press them into the bottom of the bowl. You want an uneven surface on the bottom of the bowl.

**2** Put the cooked noodles in another bowl.

**3** Mix a few drops of red and green food coloring into the milk to get a light gray color.

**4** Ask an adult to pour 125 mL (½ c.) of boiling water into a measuring cup. Add the gelatin powder. Stir quickly for about 15 seconds, until the gelatin is dissolved.

**5** Let the gelatin mixture cool slightly, but not set. Add the colored milk.

**6** Pour the gelatin mixture into the noodles and stir.

**7** Pour the noodles into the tin foil–covered bowl and pat them down well. Pour in any leftover gelatin mixture.

**8** Put your pie in the fridge for about an hour, until set.

**9** Get an adult to help you with this step. Place a plate over the bowl, hold them together firmly and tip them upside down so that the noodles are on the plate. Remove the foil and you've got BRAINS!

*TIP:* To make your brain pie look even more realistic, make 2 cuts down the center of the pie, about 0.5 cm (¼ in.) wide and 1 cm (½ in.) deep. Remove the excess noodles from the opening. Now your brain pie has 2 halves, just like a real brain.

# SHRUNKEN HEADS

Follow these instructions for a shrunken, shriveled head that looks **SHOCKINGLY REAL.** *(And we mean shockingly!)* It'll take 3 to 4 weeks to shrink completely, but it's worth the wait.

Pucker up, Honeybunch!

I'm already puckered up.

**STUFF YOU'LL NEED:**
- 1 apple, the bigger the better
- corn syrup
- hair — yours or a friend's (collect some after a haircut)
- wire and string for hanging (optional)

## SOME THINGS TO DO WITH YOUR SHRUNKEN HEAD

✱ Put it under a hat. When someone lifts the hat ...

# What to do:

**1** Peel the apple or ask an adult to do it for you. Leave a bit of skin on the top and bottom.

**2** Use a kitchen knife to carve a nose, a mouth, eyes and ears into the apple. Make these parts big because they will shrink. The carving doesn't have to be perfect — the shrinking will cover a lot of mistakes. You may want to use a toothpick to make holes for the eyes and nose and to add smaller details.

**3** Place the apple on a paper towel and put it on a windowsill or other warm spot. It may take 3 to 4 weeks to dry. If you live in a humid area, try putting it near a hot air vent.

**4** Dab a bit of corn syrup on the top of the head and stick on some hair. Do little bits at a time until you get just the right (creepy) look.

✱ Leave it on someone's pillow.

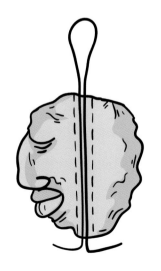

✱ Use a skewer to make a hole through the apple. Put a wire through the hole and attach a string. Then hang the head in a doorway.

29

# SEVERED FINGER

This one is such a creepy classic that we just had to include it. Sure, it's as old as the hills, but it's always new to someone ...

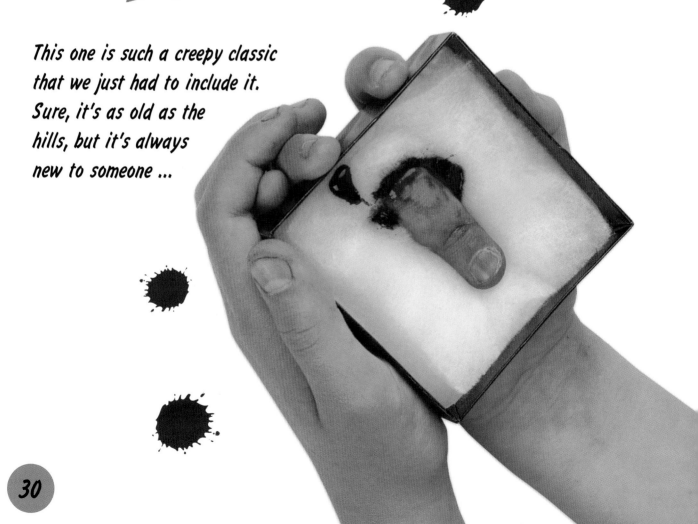

30

**TIP:** *To make your finger look as if it has been dead a long time, dip it into a mixture of 50 mL (¼ c.) water and 2 drops of blue food coloring. This will turn your finger slightly blue. Dry your blue finger and sprinkle it with baby powder. Blow off any extra powder. Now you've got a really dead-looking finger.*

# What to do:

**1** Cut a small hole in the box just big enough to stick your third finger through. The hole should go through both the cardboard and the cotton batting.

**2** Stick your finger through the hole you've made. Hold the box with your other fingers.

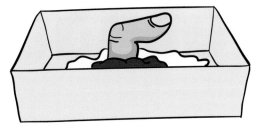

**3** Use the cotton swab to smear the fake blood at the base of your finger to make it look severed from your hand. Dab a few drops of the blood on the cotton batting around your finger.

**4** Put the lid on the box. Find someone to scare. Hold out the box (with your severed finger in place) and say, "Hey, guess what I've got!" Let your victim take the lid off. Watch the reaction!

**TIP:** *For an even grislier effect, try a severed hand. Do the same as for your finger, only use a shoe box and your whole hand.*

# BRoKEN GLASS

Have you noticed that parents really don't like it when you **BREAK THINGS**? Well, they're not going to like this stuff either, because it looks just like the real thing.

I didn't do it. HONEST!

CRASHHHHH!

32

**TIP:** Spread your 100% PURE FAKE broken glass pieces across someone's newspaper or a hard surface.

# What to do:

**1** Ask an adult to pour 50 mL (¼ c.) of boiling water into a measuring cup. Add the gelatin powder. Stir quickly for about 15 seconds, until the gelatin is dissolved. Use a spoon to skim off the bubbles and dispose of them in the garbage.

HOT LIQUIDS

**GET ADULT HELP**

**2** Pour the gelatin onto the baking tray. Swirl the tray around to get a thin layer. Let it set for about 2 hours.

**3** Use a table knife to cut your glass into different triangle shapes. Make some narrow and small, like little shards of glass, and others bigger.

NOT REALLY **FRAGILE** NOT REALLY

33

# CHOCOLATE MILK SPILL

Spilled chocolate milk can leave a big mess. Not this 100% PURE FAKE spill. It won't stain, but it WILL annoy. Be patient: It takes up to four days to dry.

Hey, Dad, don't panic! It's fake!

# What to do:

**1** In a small bowl, mix the glue and the 2 paints until you get a nice, rich chocolate color. Add a bit more brown paint, if necessary. Use a spoon to skim off the bubbles and dispose of them in the garbage.

**2** Pour the mixture into the plastic or paper cup. Place the straw in the cup and gently tip the cup on its side on the baking tray. Tip out a bit more liquid, if you wish, to make a larger spill.

**3** Let the spill set. This will take up to 4 days, depending on the temperature in your house. Make sure there are no little damp patches before you use it.

How to make the most of your FAKE SPILL

✳ Put it smack in the middle of the carpet, then leave the room and wait for the screech.

✳ Set it on someone's favorite magazine or the TV Guide.

Put one or two fake worms in a salad when no one is looking.

# SLIMY WORMS

*Worms are great in the garden, but not so great if you find them in your food — unless, of course, you like EATING them. And in this case you can!*

**STUFF YOU'LL NEED:**
- 12 or more thick straws
- a loaf tin, about 25 cm x 12 cm (10 in. x 5 in.)
- 15 mL (1 tbsp.) strawberry- or raspberry-flavored gelatin powder
- 15 mL (1 tbsp.) unflavored gelatin powder
- green food coloring
- 15 mL (1 tbsp.) milk

# What to do:

**HOT LIQUIDS**
**GET ADULT HELP**

**1** Lay the straws on the bottom of the loaf tin, lined up in a single layer. You may need to cut the ends to fit.

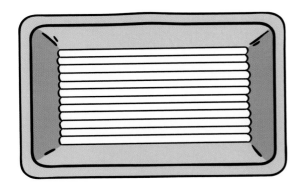

**2** Ask an adult to pour 150 mL (⅔ c.) of boiling water into a measuring cup. Add the flavored and unflavored gelatin powders. Stir quickly for about 15 seconds, until the gelatin is dissolved.

**3** Add 2 drops of green food coloring to turn your worms brown. Add the milk and stir.

**4** Let the mixture cool slightly, but not set. Then pour it over the straws in the bottom of the tin.

**5** To fill the straws with the gelatin mixture, swirl the mixture around in the tin or hold the straws down with a spoon (or your fingers if the mixture is cool enough). Keep swirling and submerging the straws until they are filled with the mixture and they don't have any air bubbles. This takes a bit of fiddling, but it's worth it.

**6** Put the tin in the fridge for an hour.

**7** Take the tin out of the fridge. Use a kitchen knife to cut between the straws so you can get them out one at a time.

**8** Remove a straw from the tin. Hold the straw under warm running water to get rid of the excess gelatin and to warm the gelatin inside slightly. Remove the straw from the running water. Hold the straw tightly at one end and run your fingers down the straw to squeeze the gelatin worm out onto a plate. Repeat with all the straws.

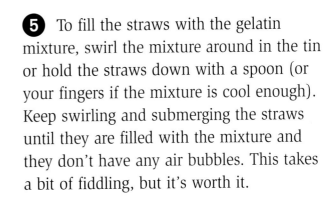

*TIP:* For even more worms, double the recipe and use a bigger pan. As long as the straws are in a single layer, it'll work.

# ROAD KILL GUTS

Everyone will *DIE* when they see this mess of guts. And the recipe is *DEAD* easy.
All it takes is an assortment of dried tubular pastas, such as spaghetti, macaroni and cannelloni.
You can also use udon noodles.

**STUFF YOU'LL NEED:**
- 3 kinds of pasta — you'll need a small handful of the long pastas and about 250 mL (1 c.) of the others
- Basic Blood (page 9) or red food coloring
- blue and green food coloring
- uncooked rice or brown-colored cereal

⚠ **HOT STOVE**

**GET ADULT HELP**

# What to do:

**1** Ask an adult to cook the dried pastas separately, according to the directions on the package, then drain them and run them under cool water. Put each kind of pasta into a separate bowl.

**2** This is where it gets a bit messy. Pour some of the Basic Blood mixture or a few drops of red food coloring into one of the pastas and mix well. Add a few drops of blue to another pasta and a few drops of green to the last pasta. Mix each bowl well. Now you have 3 different colors of pasta.

**3** Let the pastas sit for a few minutes so the color really soaks in. Then combine the 3 pastas in a resealable plastic bag and gently mix.

**4** Add a sprinkle of rice and a small handful of rolled oats or any cereal you have handy. Shake the bag until the pastas are mixed together.

## Extra special fake F/X

✱ Pour some of your guts onto the grass outside when no one is looking. Call over a friend and say, "Eeew! Look!"

✱ Try this classic — and never-fail — Halloween trick. Put your fake guts into a plastic bag. Turn off the lights. Ask people to reach in and feel them. Then flick on the lights so they can see what they've been touching.

39

# VEGGIE VOMIT

Does just LOOKING at VOMIT make you GAG? If so, you might want to pass on this stuff because it looks disgustingly like the real thing.

**STUFF YOU'LL NEED:**
- 125 mL (½ c.) applesauce
- 30 mL (2 tbsp.) unflavored gelatin
- 30 mL (2 tbsp.) uncooked rolled oats
- 125 mL (½ c.) finely chopped carrots and broccoli

# What to do:

**1** Ask an adult to heat the applesauce in a nonstick pan on medium heat until it just begins to bubble. Remove from the heat.

**2** Add the gelatin powder and stir until the gelatin is dissolved. It's okay if it's a bit lumpy.

**!**
**HOT STOVE**
*GET ADULT HELP*

**3** Add the rest of the ingredients and mix well.

**4** Pour the fake vomit onto a plate covered with waxed paper. Spread it out so that it looks like someone has vomited.

**5** Put it in the fridge to set for 1 to 2 hours. Now it's ready to use. You can store your vomit for 1 or 2 days in the fridge or freeze it for several weeks.

# Things you can do with your fake vomit

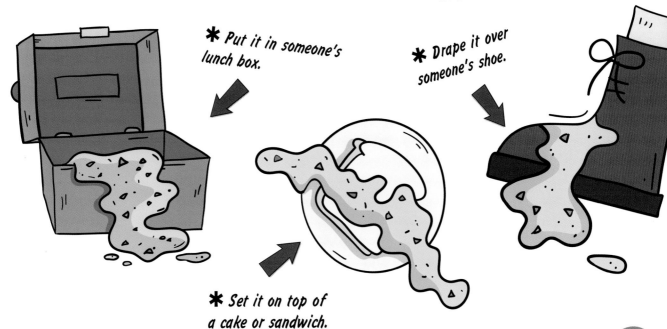

✱ *Put it in someone's lunch box.*

✱ *Drape it over someone's shoe.*

✱ *Set it on top of a cake or sandwich.*

This doesn't look quite as lifelike as the Veggie Vomit, but it's got one big advantage: You can eat it. Imagine the GROSS-OUT possibilities!

YUM!!

## STUFF YOU'LL NEED:

- 50 mL (¼ c.) applesauce
- 15 mL (1 tbsp.) unflavored gelatin powder
- 1 or 2 pinches cocoa powder
- 15 mL (1 tbsp.) uncooked rolled oats
- 15 mL (1 tbsp.) Corn Flakes or similar breakfast cereal
- 7 mL (½ tbsp.) raisins or currants

**HOT STOVE**

*GET ADULT HELP*

# What to do:

**1** Have an adult heat the applesauce in a nonstick pan on medium heat until it just begins to bubble, then remove it from the heat.

**2** Stir in the gelatin powder and keep stirring until it dissolves. Don't worry if there are some lumps.

**3** Stir in the rest of the ingredients and mix well.

**4** Turn the mixture onto a plate covered with waxed paper. Spread it out a bit and make it look like vomit.

**5** Let it set in the fridge for 1 to 2 hours, then it's ready to go. It can be stored in the fridge for 1 or 2 days or kept in the freezer for several weeks. But don't eat it after it's been frozen.

*TIP:* Keep your vomit hidden on your lap when eating with family or friends. Pretend to vomit, place the vomit in the palm of one hand and eat a chunk.

*(DO NOT EAT IT IF IT HAS BEEN ON THE FLOOR OR ANYWHERE THAT BACTERIA LINGER.)*

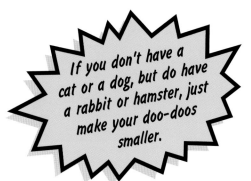

If you don't have a cat or a dog, but do have a rabbit or hamster, just make your doo-doos smaller.

# Cat AND Dog Doo-Doos

These **DOO-DOOS** look just like what comes out of the south end of your pet. But unlike the real thing, they don't smell (we can't fake everything). Note: They will take one to two days to dry.

***READ THIS:*** THESE DOO-DOOS AREN'T EDIBLE. But the ones on page 46 are. These ones look better, but the edible doo-doos have an extra shock effect that's hard to resist. Which do you like best?

**ALLERGY ALERT!!!**

*Contains cocoa*

**STUFF YOU'LL NEED:**
- 50 mL (¼ c.) salt
- 125 mL (½ c.) whole wheat flour (if using white flour, double the cocoa powder)
- 15 mL (1 tbsp.) cocoa powder
- 125 mL (½ c.) used coffee grounds
- 50 mL (¼ c.) cold coffee or water

# What to do:

**1** Mix the salt, flour and cocoa together in a bowl.

**2** Add the coffee grounds and mix well.

**3** Add the cold coffee or water and mix until you have moldable dough.

**4** Shape small handfuls of the dough into doo-doos and place them on a baking tray lined with waxed paper. Let them dry for a day or so. Enjoy!

# What to doo-doo with your fake doo-doos

**✱ Slip one or two doo-doos between a family member's bedsheets. Listen for the reaction at bedtime.**

**✱ Leave a few by the front door before you go to bed and see who finds them in the morning.**

# Edible DOO-DOOS

Here's a way to really gross out your friends. Make these YUMMY DOO-DOO cookies and then, when you have an audience, eat them.

**STUFF YOU'LL NEED:**
- 125 mL (½ c.) margarine or butter
- 125 mL (½ c.) white sugar
- 30 mL (2 tbsp.) cocoa powder
- 1 egg
- 2.5 mL (½ tsp.) vanilla flavoring
- green food coloring
- 125 mL (½ c.) packed brown sugar
- 250 mL (1 c.) flour
- 125 mL (½ c.) uncooked rolled oats
- 250 mL (1 c.) Corn Flakes, wheat flakes, shredded wheat, or other cereal

Take some to school in your LUNCH BOX and surprise your friends!

Awesome! Look what I've got for lunch!

46

**HOT STOVE**

GET ADULT HELP

**ALLERGY ALERT!!!**

Contains cocoa

# What to do:

**1** Ask an adult to preheat the oven to 190° C (375° F).

**2** In a saucepan, mix the margarine or butter, white sugar and cocoa powder together. Ask an adult to heat the mixture on the stove and stir as it melts. Remove from the heat when the mixture is completely melted. This will take about 2 minutes.

**3** In a bowl, mix the egg, vanilla and a few drops of green food coloring.

**4** Add the brown sugar to the green eggs and stir thoroughly.

**5** Gradually add the flour to the egg mixture and stir. When you've used about half the flour, add some of the melted cocoa mixture and stir. Keep adding flour and the cocoa mixture bit by bit, stirring after each addition. It will become sticky and quite hard to mix.

**6** Add the rolled oats and cereal to the mixture bit by bit. Again, it will be hard to mix. You may need to use your hands — make sure they're clean. When you're done, the mixture will look brown and chunky.

**7** Take a small amount of dough in your hands and shape it into a doo-doo. Wet your hands for easier molding. The doo-doos will flatten slightly during cooking, so make them high and round.

**8** Place the doo-doos on a lightly oiled baking tray. Leave space between them — they will spread out as they bake.

**9** Bake for about 12 minutes. Remove doo-doos from tray and place them on a rack to cool. Your doo-doos will last for 2 to 3 days if stored in a sealed container.

# PUDDLE OF PEE

*If you've got a pet, try this 100% PURE FAKE PEE. Set it by the front door or near someone's bed and watch what happens.*

**STUFF YOU'LL NEED:**
- 30 mL (2 tbsp.) unflavored gelatin powder
- yellow food coloring
- a fine paintbrush

**HOT LIQUIDS**

*GET ADULT HELP*

## What to do:

**1** Ask an adult to pour 50 mL (¼ c.) boiling water into a measuring cup. Add the gelatin powder. Stir quickly for about 15 seconds, until the gelatin is dissolved.

**2** Squeeze a drop of yellow food coloring onto a small dish. Dip the tip of the paintbrush into the food coloring and stir it into the gelatin mixture. Repeat until you have a nice pee yellow. Use a spoon to skim off the bubbles and dispose of them in the garbage.

**3** Pour the mixture onto a nonstick or slightly oiled baking tray and let the spill set. This will take up to 2 hours, depending on the temperature in your house. To speed up the process, put it in the fridge. Caution: The edges will curl up in about 24 hours, so use it before then.